Eau Claire
District Library

In Memory of

Ed Holle

THE BOOK OF
WOOD CARVING

FRONT DOOR OF THE SAYERS' HOME

THE BOOK OF
WOOD CARVING
TECHNIQUE, DESIGNS
AND PROJECTS

by

Charles Marshall Sayers

DOVER PUBLICATIONS, INC.
NEW YORK

Published in Canada by General Publishing
Company, Ltd., 30 Lesmill Road, Don Mills,
Toronto, Ontario.
Published in the United Kingdom by Con-
stable and Company, Ltd., 10 Orange Street,
London WC2H 7EG.

This Dover edition, first published in 1978,
is an unabridged republication of the work
originally published by The Caxton Printers,
Ltd., Caldwell, Idaho, in 1942 under the
title *The Book of Wood Carving: A Text for
Beginners*. A new Preface has been written and
various textual emendations have been made
especially for this edition.

International Standard Book Number:
0-486-23654-4
Library of Congress Catalog Card Number:
78-52156

Manufactured in the United States of America
Dover Publications, Inc.
31 East 2nd Street
Mineola, N.Y. 11501

Preface to the Dover Edition

CHARLES Marshall Sayers was born on December 21, 1892, in Kirkcudbright, Scotland, one of the oldest seaports in Britain and the birthplace of John Paul Jones. He was the tenth of thirteen children. When he was seven his father, James Charles Sayers, bought him some wood-carving tools. Since there was no one to instruct him, he learned by trial and error, aided by an inborn sensitivity to what could be done with these tools. Within a short time the feel of the tools in his hands told him that wood carving was to become his prime and lasting interest.

When he was thirteen his family moved to The Stell, a property outside of Kirkcudbright near the River Dee. Charles refused to attend the Academy, the next school in line for him. Instead he apprenticed himself to his father, who, although not a wood-carver, was a master craftsman in woodwork. His training progressed through the various forms of woodwork to fine-furniture making. This instruction was interspersed with boat building, Kirkcudbright being an active port for fishermen.

Charles was fourteen when his relief-carved portrait of the world champion Clydesdale Baron's Pride received a first award in an art exhibition in Kirkcudbright. At that time he also had his first experience in teaching, his first student being one of his former school teachers.

Several years later he went to Glasgow to attend the Royal Technical College, specializing and winning two awards in furniture, design and detail. He also attended the School of Art, where he studied sculpture and figure drawing. To enable himself to continue his studies he worked in the shipyards. When the First World War broke out he enlisted in the Royal Field Artillery, becoming one of Kitchener's First Hundred Thousand. He was sent to the Somme and later to the Balkans. After the Armistice he returned to Kirkcudbright, his left side disabled as the result of injury and exposure. Through sheer determination and effort he recovered the use of his left arm and hand, walked again without a cane and regained his facility in wood carving.

In 1924 Sayers came to the United States to visit his elder brother and his family, who were living in Seattle. Sensing wider opportunities in this country, he never returned to Scotland. He remained in Seattle for several years, began to teach carving and accepted orders for just about anything in woodwork that came his way.

Four years later, on a visit to California, he saw Carmel and knew that this was where he had to live, finding in the colony of artists, craftsmen and writers an atmosphere such as he had known in Kirkcudbright. He established his studio and workshop under the name of The School of Woodcarving. In due time, word of his ability as a wood carver, furniture maker, designer and teacher began to travel. His students and those interested in his work were composed not only of people from the immediate area, but also of visitors who came regularly to Carmel for their vacations or for the express purpose of study with him.

Though busy, those building years were difficult ones. In 1929 Sayers found himself one of the many trying to work their way out of the worldwide Depression. In 1930 he began building his own home in Carmel, doing most of the work himself. The two-story rustic house, set among Carmel's pine trees, boasted carvings inside and out that reflected the old-world feeling that touched all his work. As a result of the first article about his home and work, he and his wife, Cecily, entertained many unexpected visitors there.

It was during the early thirties that he formed his first class in San Francisco, at the request of a group of teachers employed by the public school system. Some wanted to include wood carving in their craft classes; others wanted to teach it in classes intended specifically for mentally handicapped children. The response of the children who became involved was rewarding.

Sayers' teaching duties began to take him farther afield, to Colorado and Iowa; but in 1941 he began to cut down on these activities as he became more involved in exhibiting carvings in various flower shows and exhibitions. In the same year he and his wife moved, briefly, to San Francisco. In 1942, they settled in Walnut Creek, at that time a comparatively drowsy town in Contra Costa County, where he had been invited to join the new Art and Garden Center which was being developed. Once established, Sayers taught the construction of fine furniture to those interested in incorporating wood carving into this demanding craft. Using an absolute minimum of power equipment, the enthusiastic students constructed the furniture almost entirely by hand, as Sayers had been doing for years.

In 1946 he moved to Alamo, a few miles south of Walnut Creek. In the foothills rising above the San Ramon Valley he established his school and his home. It was there that he once more enhanced home and garden with wood carving. The softly tinted block buildings with their shake roofs soon settled into the landscape.

A few years later he gave up his exhibits at the California Spring Garden Show. He had taken part each year since 1941, enjoying the challenge that it had presented. But he could no longer spare the time for it and, with few exceptions, he ceased to concern himself with future exhibits of any nature.

He was satisfied to be active within his own surroundings until a stroke made it necessary to give up his classes and, by degrees, his own carving. He died May 10, 1971.

Slightly under six feet, he was a powerful man whose intense blue eyes betrayed a lurking humor, even before he spoke. He had a passion for work—his own kind of work. Although he delighted in the conviviality of friends, there was much of the hermit in this man who, as happens with most creative people, required more quietude than he was able to find. He was never the one for much fanfare, but his own craftsmanship and skill as a teacher had progressive influence on the growth of interest in the art of wood carving.

From material provided by Cecily Sayers

TO
CECILY
My Wife

Charles Marshall Sayers.

I WISH to express my sincere gratitude to Miss Rachel Beiser, who has worked faithfully in typing and correcting this manuscript. Anyone knowing my handwriting would suggest giving Miss Beiser a medal for being able to make anything of my dreadful scrawl.

Also, my sincere appreciation to Francis Whitaker and to Horace D. Lyon for their co-operation in the photography for this book.

CHARLES MARSHALL SAYERS.

Preface to the First Edition

THERE seems to be a crying need for a sound elementary text book on wood carving, and after much thought and many expressions of encouragement on the part of my students, I have decided to put down as plainly as possible, and with as little technical phraseology as is essential to sound teaching, the first steps for the average person with no previous experience.

This is not written with the idea of training professionals — in fact, my methods are quite unorthodox, but have the advantage over the older style, in that the results are more rapid, and have a freer and less stilted technique.

Foreword

HERE is an interesting book. In fact, it is the best book for beginners on the fascinating art of wood carving that I have seen. It is written in such a clear, crisp, and concise manner that all wood workers, who heretofore have looked upon wood carving as being too difficult to attempt, will discover a new conception of its possibilities and will have the urge to do some of the type of carving shown and described so graphically in this book.

First of all, Mr. Sayers recommends the use of but four tools, all of which are large enough to be handled easily by the beginner. Secondly, the designs which he recommends are of the flowing type, very decorative in character, upon which progress is made rapidly and the beginner is encouraged by his success instead of being discouraged as is the case with carvings with intricate detail. Thirdly, the modeling is of a type which brings out the highlights and shadows, always highly desirable in all types of wood carving. The excellent photographs illustrate this point much better than any description that I might give.

A visit to the Sayers' home in Carmel is indeed a refreshing experience where one can see wood carving at its best, created and executed in good taste in both interior and exterior decoration. In this setting are to be found beautiful examples of woods finished in such a manner that the natural beauty is retained and emphasized.

In using any medium creatively, whether it is wood, metal, clay, or textile, two vital elements confront the beginner—design and craftsmanship. Which of these two elements should be considered first is naturally a debatable question. I have the feeling that we must know the limitations of the tools and materials which are being used to understand the possibilities of the design. But good design is fundamental and essential in all creative work if the finished product is to possess merit and value as well as beauty.

I recommend this book most heartily to all industrial arts teachers who wish to create a more interesting approach to their work, to all home shop workers who naturally experiment with tools and materials, and to all men, women, and children who seek an emotional release through some form of creative expression.

R. C. WOOLMAN
Director, Industrial Education
Des Moines Public Schools
Des Moines, Iowa

February 7, 1939

Table of Contents

List of Illustrations

THE BOOK OF
WOOD CARVING

Introduction

THERE is a keen joy in creative work, and from primitive times, when our ancestors scratched on bone and ivory, making crude outlines of lions, elephants, and hunting scenes, through all the ages, we have tried to express ourselves in various mediums.

The man on the street, though appreciative of the magnificent carvings in public buildings, passenger liners, and cathedrals, is more keenly interested in the application of this craft to objects in everyday use.

It is not my intention to go into wood sculpture in this book, but it is the most difficult of the mediums, and the highest form of sculpture. The amateur at anything, will, at times, hold his own with the professional, when it comes to results, but usually his methods are more intricate in arriving, and the time occupied out of all proportion to the work involved.

In teaching, I always try to avoid interfering in any way with original ideas, but strive to develop sound technique. One can get good results with a pocketknife. I ought to know, having done pierced carving as a boy with that instrument, but it is something like making fire with a rubbing stick when you have a box of matches in your pocket. No matter what you are desirous of accomplishing ultimately in carving, begin with simple, conventional design, preferably on the geometric order. And my reason for saying so is that thereby you learn to cut wood to stated lines. In other words, you learn control of the instruments, and material, to know the grain, and how to cut with it, not fighting the wood, but always getting the best results with the least possible effort.

This talk of art and genius is mostly haverin'. A good artist is first a good workman. That almost invariably applies. When speaking of wood carving, that does not mean scratching on toothbrush racks, or match boxes, but sound, sane ornament applied conservatively to furniture and woodwork.

I fear I do not suffer fools gladly, for when someone inquires how many lessons it takes to enable one to make a livelihood at wood carving, I just glower, and reply that I have been more than thirty years at the game, and can't yet make a livelihood, which usually does the trick.

To me it seems that most people spend too much time theorizing, and in a somewhat crowded life, in which I have done almost all things in woodwork, from cradles to coffins, and such varied things as sculpture, painting, and acting, I have found that practice, assisted by theory, is best. I never did like the word *can't*. It is such a useless and irritating word. Make up your mind to do a thing, and granted you are prepared to make the necessary sacrifice, nine times out of ten you reach your goal.

Many of you will find that you have not the feeling for wood sculpture. But, after all, so few have the aptitude, why worry, when there is so much genuine satisfaction in carving a chest, a bed, or a coffee table so that they make a home distinctive. There is pleasure when you put on your slippers of an evening, and rest your feet on the hob, to feel not only the glow of the fire, but that grand inward glow as your gaze rests on a mantel you have carved.

What if it isn't figures in bas-relief? Conventional ornament can be very satisfactory.

When you open your door to arriving guests, think of the thrill when they exclaim about the carved door; and if you have picked up the door for a dollar, as I did mine, the thrill is only greater to think you have made a thing of beauty at so little cost. That does not mean you should carve everything in the house. It is a real virtue to know when to stop, but if the right designs are chosen, a lot can be used without a feeling of being overdone.

Then the outdoors; so much can be done with window facings, verge boards, gateways, patio furniture such as carved outdoor benches and tables, especially if you live in California where it is always sunny, and fog is very unusual. For these, of course, the carving should be bold and strongly cut, so that it will carry in the light of outdoors.

Frequently it is not so much that carving is poor, but that it is out of proportion to the space it is intended to ornament, or it is misplaced. It is a common misconception that shallow wood carving is more easily executed. On the contrary, a greater amount of skill is necessary, and defects will usually show more clearly. It is important that the depth be in proportion to the design and to the place in which it is to be used.

A border on a table, or chest top, for example, should be confined to shallow cutting. And speaking of a border on table or chest tops, it is a practice to be avoided if possible, preference being given to well-marked woods, as the carving in such a border is difficult to keep clean.

For heaven's sake, keep away from small detail to begin with. Train the eye and hand to long swinging curves, to get the feel of the wood. Later get down to miniatures if you wish, and you will find that you maintain the same touch.

To get the feeling for wood carving design, one should endeavor to forget line drawing, and to visualize the mass. In a nutshell, the whole thing depends on the values of light and shade. For example, if for any reason it is necessary to place a head, we shall say, at a considerable elevation, one might think that the usual treatment given for use at eye level would suffice, but if tested, it will readily be seen that the whole effect is blurred and shapeless. By strong use of planes on all rounded surfaces, the light will be caught and the object appear as it would if given the ordinary treatment, and seen at eye level.

One should consider also, the distance at which the work will generally be seen; its proportion to the piece on which it is executed and the surroundings.

The Swiss do very sound carving. But in many cases it is a waste of effort, a mass of intricate detail, without meaning or suitability to the article as a whole.

The practical uses must be considered. One should avoid doing intricate, undercut carving where the head rests on a chair back, or the foot on a foot stretcher.

Try to keep the feeling of your wood. Why try to imitate stone or metal? Make your design suitable to that particular wood. Dense tough-grained woods can stand delicate execution, but for the coarse-fibred, strong, crude cutting is more appropriate. Do not misunderstand the meaning of the word "crude." It is here applied in the sense of strong, bold cutting, not rough, careless effects.

When a boy, I started in carving from nature, a branch of a beech or oak tree. It was wonderful training, if poor design. The application was so sadly out of keeping that it still hurts me to think of it, and I do believe that if I have any enemies in Britain, they have possessed themselves of my earliest pieces, and are holding them as a club over me. But carving from nature taught me to observe, and today, the masses of different types of trees are distinctive because of that early concentration.

In selecting pieces or designs for wood carving, one should first consider their suitability, especially for a house, that one can live with them. I should be proud to possess, for instance, one of the old, life-size saints, which were so often splendidly carved. However, I think I would want a gallery to keep it in. There are few homes that could quite live up to a wooden saint, not to mention a live one. Frequently you will see a large piece of furniture, of fine workmanship, good wood and well carved, but so completely out of proportion to the space in the average home that no matter how cheaply it could be obtained, its purchase would be a mistake. Plaques and fragments also can be easily overdone, unless they can be incorporated with a practical piece of furniture. Many have the knack of picking up old capitals, bolsters, brackets, et cetera, and in building, plan places for them. Used in this way there is a value, but merely to clutter up a house with bits, no matter how attractive, is a weakness.

It is somewhat difficult to lay down hard and fast rules as to how to judge good or bad wood carving. The workmanship may be excellent, and yet, because of poor design or unsuitability of application, anyone with good taste would fight shy of it. Again the workmanship may be indifferent from a mechanical viewpoint, but if correctly proportioned may be very interesting, the effect being either naive, or having a primitive quality.

There is, generally, and rightly, a prejudice against applied carving. Often this consists of bandsawed outlines, touched here and there with a gouge and glued on a perfectly flat surface. That is bad. However, in building up the high point on a Florentine frame, for instance, there can be no reasonable objection to the use. If properly fitted and glued, there is no difference from the solid wood, and a great deal of material and labor can be saved, without in any way detracting from the value of the finished work.

In one of the army riding schools was a rhyme that read something like this:

> "Your head and heart keep up;
> Your hands and heels keep down;
> Your legs close to your horse's side;
> Your elbows to your own."

Now that applies to horsemanship; but in wood carving, I would say, not being a poet, keep both hands behind the cutting edge of the tool, and do not cut towards the body, or you stand a chance of removing your appendix.

WOOD CARVER'S SLOGAN

Cut with the grain, and strop frequently!

CORRECT POSITION OF HANDS IN HOLDING TOOLS

Position of Hands in Holding Tools

LEFT hand with thumb pointing upward on handle, and the lower part well down to point of tool.

Right hand with forefinger and thumb pointing downward, and end of handle snuggled partly into the palm.

The forefinger should not be on handle, but alongside, and all fingers should be around handle or blade, firmly but freely. The heel of the left hand should rest on the wood.

While the position of the hand is the same on the different tools, it will be found in using the parting tool that if the tool is elevated to an angle, that would cause the tool to cut deeper, as the stroke is made. Then to counteract that by a slight uplift of the fingers of the left hand, the result will be to eliminate friction of metal behind the cutting edge, thus saving effort, and lessening any roughing tendency on curves. With the gouges, on the contrary, the pressure on the tool burnishes the wood, leaving a desirable clean-cut sheen to the work.

The student should avoid stooping over. Rather slump the trunk on hips, and head on shoulders, left leg advanced and both knees bent. It will be found that the feet and legs play an important part, and the body should be balanced at all times. Generally the body weight is back of all cuts, keeping the arm, at any angle, a part of the body rather than working independently. Careless posture means rapidly tiring muscles, and consequently poor work.

The use of a mallet should be avoided at first, having a tendency to make cramped work. Later, on hard woods, it is quite permissable, and almost necessary at times. When cutting with the assistance of the mallet, the tool should be held fairly loosely. This lessens the chance of breaking the cutting edge should the mallet glance off the handle of the tool, or hard grain be encountered.

Cultivating the use of both hands is of great advantage, as one can change to cut the grain, without having to move the work on hand.

Position of Tools on Bench

Have the tools on bench with points toward work. This seems to be awkward for the beginner, but a little practice shows the advantage. Pick a tool up with the left hand. ready to use. Lay it down with the same hand. This lessens the danger of cuts, and increases the speed of selection and handling.

Tools

For preparatory work, I limit my students to four tools, consisting of:

London Style

1 straight parting tool - - ½″ No. 39
                                            (or ⅜″ or ⅝″ of same number)
1 straight gouge - - - - ⅝″ No. 5
1 straight gouge - - - - 1″ No. 3
                                              (or ⅞″ of same number)
1 straight gouge - - - - ⅜″ No. 7

Later, for relief carving, it will be advantageous to have a straight gouge, ⅜″ No. 3 (see Design No. 8).

English tools, Henry Taylor's "Acorn" Professional Line, are recommended as being the finest steel. Their shapes are a development of hundreds of years of craftsmanship and expert workmanship, the balance and temper being of correct quality for the purpose of each tool. These tools can be purchased through dealers, such as many of the better art-supply shops. Request that these tools be ground sharp. If there is difficulty in obtaining them, contact Pentalic Corp., 132 W. 22nd Street, New York, New York 10013. You can ask for a quotation or for their price list catalog. If, for some reason, you must substitute, use tools of the same shape as those shown, or as similar as possible. Good steel, such as is used in Taylor tools, is an absolute necessity. Keep in mind that to try to

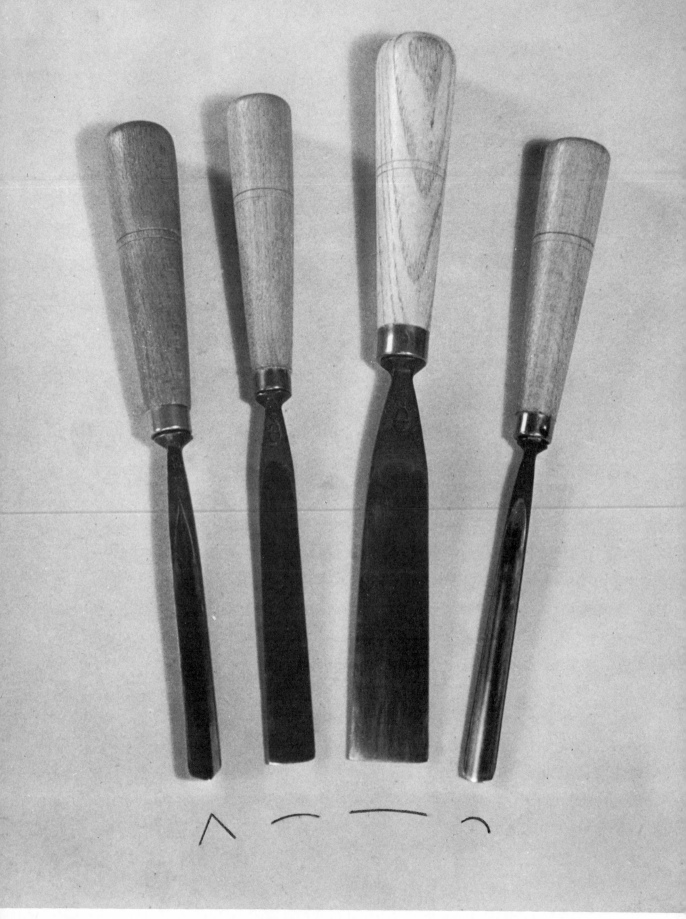

½″ No. 39, Straight Parting Tool   1″ No. 3, Straight Gouge
⅝″ No. 5, Straight Gouge   ⅜″ No. 7, Straight Gouge

save money on wood carving tools is to waste it. Should you purchase a set of tools, know the quality you are buying, as you can pay dearly for both inferior steel and packaging. The Henry Taylor "Acorn" Sets, though somewhat smaller than Taylor Professional tools, are the same quality.

One of the most important things in wood carving is the correct sharpening of tools, and I think it is better to give full instruction at this time on the care and upkeep.

A piece of leather belting is very suitable for stropping; one edge can be shaped to take the inside of the parting tool, and another rounded for the inside of the smaller gouges.

The slip stone is a hard Arkansas AS22 C. T. Slip.

A large stone is advised, as well as the slip. India Stone No. 29 Combination IB6 is recommended.

Oils recommended for use on the stone are sperm or neatsfoot.

The parting, or V tool, is the most generally used in my method, and is sharpened as follows:

Hold the tool as shown (pictured here with straight gouge), and with a firm and steady stroke, move back and forward on the stone, doing both sides until a slight roughness is felt on the inner sides. Next tilt the tool from both sides, about one-sixteenth of an inch and hold at about a twenty-degree angle and repeat sharpening until the point formed at the intersection of sides is sharp. Next take the slip stone at an angle of about one fourth of an inch in the length of the slip, and move lightly on both inner sides of the parting tool, until a slight bevel is formed. The tool should then be stropped briskly inside and out, until all trace of feather edge—as the rough wire-like edge made by the whetstone is called—has gone. Make cuts of various depths across grain on a soft piece of

CORRECT WAY OF HOLDING TOOL, AND CORRECT ANGLE TO OILSTONE

CORRECT ANGLE WHEN USING SLIPSTONE

wood. Pine is generally used. If the cuts made are smooth and without ragged scratches, the tool may be considered fit for use.

It will be noticed that a point is formed at the intersection of the two sides. This should be retained, as it helps to keep the tool in the groove and gives a cleaner cut.

Gouges are sharpened from side to side (diagram) with a rolling movement, the angle to the stone being the same as for a parting tool. Then the rounded edge of the slip is used on the inside, also with a side movement, the angle for the slip being about eight degrees, or one-fourth inch elevation in the length of the slip.

In grinding and sharpening carving tools, a different principle to that used for cabinet chisels is employed. Instead of the straight grind, and straight sharpening angle, with the tool perfectly flat on the face, for carving tools, a series of angles is preferable. The slight angle on the face breaks the shaving, acting like the cap on a plane iron.

The cutting edges of both parting tools and gouges should be at right angles to the wood surface when the tool is held in the cutting position. In other words, if, when the tool is held at the correct cutting angle, the square end of a strip of wood were placed against the cutting edges, the whole edge would touch.

Incised Carving

FOR the first lesson, work on a panel 1″ x 10″ x 14″ is recommended. This may be one of several woods, but Philippine Mahogany is very suitable, being comparatively soft, and yet having enough decided grain to compel careful cutting in the correct directions, and to teach control. Draw design shown in accompanying sketch, on board, and fix same to work bench. The bench height should be about thirty-eight inches. Fix board down with cleats nailed around the four sides. This enables one to reverse the panel, and facilitates cutting. Hold parting tool as shown in photograph, at an angle of about thirty-five degrees, and proceed to cut around outlines to a depth of about 3/16 inches. Take care not to tilt tool sideways, but to keep it even all the way through, on an even keel, as a sailor would say. Next cut center lines in leaves, starting shallow and quickly reaching a depth of about ¼ inch, then coming to the surface before quite reaching the opposite end of leaf. This line is close to one side of the leaf. Take the ⅝″ gouge No. 5, and proceed to hollow the wider side, cutting from the outer edge to almost the bottom of the center parting tool cut. It will be necessary to change the direction of the cut to suit the grain of the wood. Only practice will accustom the carver to know when to change direction. When cutting with gouges across the grain of the wood, the higher point

FIRST LESSON

should be kept slightly ahead of the lower. This will leave a cleaner surface.

When the gouge cutting is complete, take the large gouge, hollow side up, and slope the opposite side, cutting from the high center down to almost the bottom of the outer V. Cut around the center circle with parting tool, about ¼ inch deep, and slope away from outer to inner circle, using a large gouge. Then starting shallow from the outside circle, cut each straight line to form petals with parting tool, in three directions, thus making rounded corners. Later this can be done with the ⅝″ gouge hollow side down, but for a beginning, practice with the parting tool is important. Take ⅝″ gouge No. 5, and hollow petals as shown, leaving a ridge between cuts. In starting gouge cut, hold tool almost perpendicular and flatten out as you proceed with the cutting. This will give what is termed "dish" to the petals.

Now round over the center ball. The flat gouge is used for rounded surfaces, hollow side up, until one is proficient. Then frequently it will be advantageous to use it the other way. Should the beginner not feel sufficiently confident to go ahead with the next lesson, it is wise to practice carving similar leaves and flowers until sufficient accuracy is obtained, but avoid fussy, too exact cutting. The desired effect is that of bold, easy cuts, rather than mechanical perfection.

The rosette formed in this first panel is the beginning of conventional flower forms such as the Tudor rose, and has great value in wood-carving design. The leaf form in this same panel is a base for many types of leaves and scrolls.

This is known as incised carving, where the outline is followed and the background not removed. This particular style can be used successfully on panels where shallow and primitive designs are required.

This first panel, if fairly successful, can be used for the top of a small footstool, or if reduced in thickness to 9/16 of an inch, can make the front or back of a guest-book cover.

The simpler type of book cover is made by boring two holes through the front and back covers, about 3 inches from either end and ½ inch from the edge, the holes being made to take easily strips of rawhide.

The paper filler is made by folding sheets somewhat smaller than the covers, and punching holes in line with the holes in the covers. So-called butcher paper, generally known in the trade as "screenings," is very suitable. The edges of the paper should be torn over a sharp edge of wood or metal, instead of being cut. This gives a better effect.

For the purposes of study, Designs Nos. 1-6 should measure no less than 2½″ to 3″ vertically, excluding borders.

Design No. 1

SECOND LESSON

The second lesson is in the main a repetition of the methods in the first, but with a different application.

This design is suitable for borders, aprons of tables, and chair and bench rails.

First cut the border lines with the parting tool, taking care to cut to the inner side of the line, leaving borders intact. Next, cut around the arcs, cutting outside and inside lines to leave the border intact. The reason for this will be obvious, as the line remains, whereas if the cut were made down the line itself, one could be at

DESIGN NO. 1

DESIGN NO. 2

DESIGN NO. 3

either side and have no check. A parting tool cut should then be made down the straight center line, starting shallow at the top, and to the full depth of the tool at the bottom. Next, slope both sides down almost to the bottom of the parting tool cut, as shown in the accompanying plate on the page opposite, using the large flat gouge. For the curved lines shown, use the parting tool. Start shallow and cut deeply toward the finish. Take the 5/8″ gouge and cut as shown around the arc, pushing home with one cut of the tool, then using the edge of the tool to cut off chips. This method should be studied closely as it is used all through this type of carving.

Make three intersecting cuts with the parting tool in triangles between arcs, starting shallow, and deepening to the intersection, then slope away all three sides. Make a cut at center of all three sides with the parting tool, then round as in the petals on the first panel. To finish, use the 5/8″ gouge on the inside of the arc, sloping down to bottom of cut, then round over outside edge with flat gouge.

Design No. 2

THIRD LESSON

Design No. 2 introduces the use of scrolls, and it is very necessary to exert the utmost care in good curves and graceful, swinging lines. This design can be used for borders, rails, frames, barge boards, door and window facings, and is equally good on a small or fairly large scale.

Cut straight parting tool lines, taking care not to encroach on borders, then cut around scrolls and along connecting line between. Next slope both sides of connecting line, almost to bottom of cut.

Follow concave side of scrolls with the ⅝″ gouge, sloping from fully halfway on surface, almost to the bottom of the parting tool cut. Round other side over with flat gouge. Draw lines diverging from center of main line, then cut with the parting tool, deepening toward the border. On approaching end of cut, deepen, thus lessening the chances of slipping, also giving a better effect.

With the ⅝″ gouge then hollow concave sides of cuts, and round the convex, as shown in the accompanying plate. When cutting off the chip formed by the gouge against a straight line, cut off with the flat gouge. The triangle between scrolls is cut with a parting tool, and smoothed off with a flat gouge. The method all through is similar to the first panel, but the different application gives an effect of richness. It will be seen that contrasting light and shade is the whole problem, and clean-cut work, with definite bold cutting, decided hollows, and rounds that connect a series of slopes, rather than too smoothly rounded, will give a feeling of life to the article.

Design No. 3

FOURTH LESSON

Before using the text for this example, the student will undoubtedly benefit by trying to follow the steps shown in the accompanying plate, and only if unable to do so should reference be made to the written description of the procedure.

With the parting tool, cut both border lines, as in previous examples, then the main curve, these to be cut fairly deeply. Slope both sides of this cut with the large flat gouge. Next, draw in the curved lines branching from the main stem, and cut with the parting tool. Try to swing gradually from the stem, the cut gradually deepening toward the border, and when the parting tool is almost touching the border cut, raise the right hand slightly. This deepens the cut at the finish, and lessens the chances of running into the border. Next use the 5⁄8″ gouge and, commencing from the border end, cut the concave sides of the lines, carrying the cut about two-thirds across, and shallowing as the parting tool cut becomes shallower. With the large flat gouge, slope away the opposite side. Finally, with the 5⁄8″ gouge cut hollow at the border end of each member.

Design No. 4

FIFTH LESSON

Cut border lines with the parting tool, making fairly shallow cuts. Then follow curved lines with a deeper cut, being careful to swing easily from the border line, and easily into the other. Hollow the sides away from the center, using the 5⁄8″ gouge, and cutting about two-thirds across. At the upper ends, it will be seen that a slight triangle is formed, giving a return to the point of the leaf. This is made with the parting tool, cutting from both ends. Next round off the opposite side of the leaf with the large flat gouge. The center leaf is sloped away on both sides.

In Designs Nos. 1, 2, 3, and 4 you will find the same build-up, with occasional additions, and generally, the same type of cutting, as they are planned to improve the technique.

All these pieces can be applied into useful articles and pieces of furniture.

DESIGN NO. 4

DESIGN NO. 5

DESIGN NO. 6

The beginner will profit greatly by endeavoring to work out each design until the result has something of the character shown in the examples.

It is well to mention here the importance of keeping the tools sharp, and they should be stropped frequently, thus keeping the edge from dulling so rapidly, as well as the gain to the work on hand. Cutting with the grain of the wood will come with practice, and while it is possible to cut against the grain with many woods, and at times this is unavoidable, whenever possible, avoid this, as the wood has a poorer surface compared with the silky texture when properly treated.

Designs Nos. 5 and 6

SIXTH LESSON

In addition to the designs already specified, I would like to add a simple treatment which is very effective, and at the same time wonderfully good for control.

Do not follow the border lines with the parting tool as in the other examples, but cut with the parting tool only at lines heavily drawn, starting shallow, and cutting deeply to intersection, then sloping all sides from fine lines to bottom of cuts, using flat gouge for slopes. On surfaces between triangles, in Design No. 5, cut a groove with the ⅜″ gouge, slightly rounding intersections.

At no time should any attempt be made at too precise cutting. Slight irregularities of surface, provided the cuts are cleanly done, will in no way mar, but rather improve the appearance of the finished piece. Throughout all this type of wood carving, in none of

DESIGN NO. 7

which background appears, avoid, when modelling, cutting to the bottom of the parting tool cuts, as a certain amount of the latter will emphasize the shadows, and the labor involved is much less. This, of course, does not apply to Designs Nos. 5 and 6.

For Designs Nos. 7, 8, and 9 it is advisable at first to keep the original measurements of the panels shown: ½″ or 1″ x 10″ x 14″.

Design No. 7

SEVENTH LESSON

Before starting on relief carving, I should state that there are times when the type of carving shown in Design No. 7 can be used to great advantage. This panel shown here is very suitable for a guest-book cover.

The method of carving is as follows: Cut around the outlines of figures, foliage, etc., with the parting tool to the depth required. Next model to the desired effect, and finally with the large flat gouge, tool all the background, and slope away the parting tool cuts to meet the background. The result will give a feeling not unlike hammered metal in texture, and provided the application is appropriate to the work being executed, very satisfactory effects can be obtained.

Relief Carving

Design No. 8

EIGHTH LESSON

Now for relief carving. To begin with, we will use scrolls as shown in Design No. 8. These will necessitate long sweeps of the tools, and unless they are clearly executed, will lose character.

In wood carving, designs that appear very intricate are very frequently the least difficult, as mistakes are more easily remedied or concealed. Simple curves call for sound technique, and errors will show plainly. In the early stages avoid small cramped work, as this tends to finicky cutting, and the workmanship suffers accordingly. Try to make every cut tell, and the result will merit the labor involved.

Draw on a panel the design shown. Cut around the border with the parting tool, taking care to cut the lines crossing the grain first, as the tool is more easily controlled. Always start the cut a little from the corner, afterward cutting back to the corner from the other direction, thus avoiding marks of the tool on the border. The border side of the cut should be carefully watched. The other is not so important, as it will cut away later. When this is done, follow the outlines of the design, again leaving the pencil line just showing, which means that you cut outside of the scroll or whatever design you have in hand.

DESIGN NO. 8

The older method was to cut entirely outside the line with the parting tool, and then with chisels or gouges to suit the line or curves, cut straight, or almost straight down with the aid of a mallet. To cut directly for finished effect with the parting tool, except in cramped curves or corners, gives a freedom to the work, and avoids stilted technique. When the outline is completed, use the ⅝" gouge and cut across all background to almost the depth of the parting tool cut. Here is a good place to practice steady strokes, and to bring the tool to a stop at any place desired. It will be seen that the gouge cuts are on a slight angle across grain, and the reason for this will be seen when the student reaches this stage. Try a few straight cuts across, then at a slight angle, and the difference in the ease of cutting will be clearly discernible.

Having removed the background as shown, the process being termed "roughing in," take the large flat gouge, 1" No. 3, and remove rough edges adjoining the parting tool cuts. With suitable gouge, cut outlines in cramped corners. Model design as shown. The student should have no difficulty in following this process, the routine being similar to previous panels. Be careful, however, to leave a definite edge of at least 1/16 of an inch between where the modelling finishes, and the background. This casts a shadow and gives a greater feeling of depth to the work.

When the modelling is satisfactorily completed, take the 1" No. 3 gouge, and, with the hollow side upward, proceed to smooth off the background, usually at an angle across the grain. It will be necessary to vary the procedure according to the wood and to the type of design. Difficulty may be experienced in cleaning into cramped spaces, and the student may find it necessary to purchase an extra tool for this. The tool required is a ⅜" No. 3 gouge. In smoothing up background, be careful to remove all parting tool cuts, the desired effect being that of the background disappearing behind the design.

In the older style carving, a method called "lazy man's background" was resorted to. But being utterly mechanical, and, as the name implies, an excuse for poor workmanship, its use is condemned. It is well, however, to describe it. The background is roughly cleaned up, and a tool named a punch, in other words, a piece of metal with a number of sharp points on one end, is used to cover the whole surface, making innumerable small holes. This covers all minor defects of cutting, but the result is monotonous and not to be advocated.

Design No. 9

For a more intricate stage of relief carving, I suggest a Tudor rose and foliage as shown in Design No. 9.

The procedure is similar to the previous example. But in cutting the leaves, at first disregard the indentations, and simply follow the general outlines. Rough out the background, and model leaves by cutting with the parting tool along center line. Then with the 5/8" gouge, slope inward from both sides. Take the same gouge, or a 3/8" gouge, and at an angle from the center, make varying depth cuts to and through the outside edge, trying to avoid sameness. With the parting tool held almost straight upright, cut indentations, and with the flat gouge, soften off some of the sharp angles.

Where the stems cross, do not cut until the background is removed, then vary the depth of cuts at intersection, afterward sloping

Method for Cutting Design No. 10

DESIGN No. 10 is very suitable for table aprons, or rails. Care should be taken to cut with parting tool on upper line only, and cutting should be quite shallow. With parting tool, cut center lines, finishing cuts to either end, but deepening quickly at top. Then roughly round corners, finishing with large flat gouge. At the bottom of hollows, use ⅝" gouge. If the design is large, two cuts may be necessary. Hold gouge with hollow side toward body on a distinct angle. This leaves a sloping edge, giving strength, and holding the light. It may be necessary for better effect to use a number seven gouge for this purpose, first cutting down the center from the top, then easing away to either side.

If Designs Nos. 10-14 are carved on one panel, as shown, the panel should measure no less than 8" vertically.

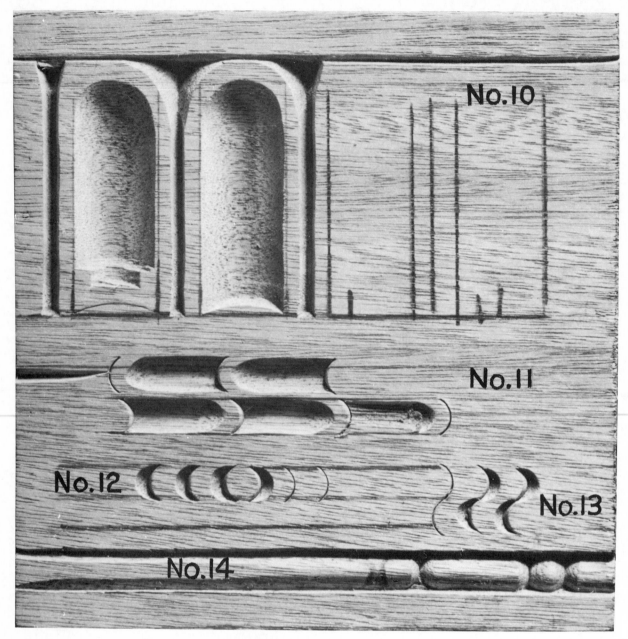

DESIGNS NOS. 10, 11, 12, 13, AND 14

Method for Cutting Designs
Nos. 11, 12, 13, and 14

In cutting Designs Nos. 11-14, care should be taken in making the first gouge cut, holding the tool as given in directions for cutting No. 10. For No. 14, *the ball-and-bead mould*, draw two lines which are a fraction wider apart than the width of the ⅜″ gouge. Cut inside the lines with the parting tool, in each case tilting tool toward the center.

With the ⅜″ gouge, hollow side down, round the ridge formed by the parting tool cuts. It may be necessary to sharpen the ⅜″ gouge at a greater angle from the inside, to prevent the tool from cutting down into the wood too much. Next mark off the position for the balls, still using tool with hollow side down. Round over from center of ball, cutting fairly deeply with a rounding movement. The end of the beads are treated the same way. The parting tool can be used to clean corners at gouge intersections.

In a number of the following designs, the details of carving methods employed have purposely been omitted. If the previous exercises have been faithfully worked out, the student should have no difficulty in following the various steps to be taken. The plates should be studied carefully.

My reason for avoiding description is to encourage the student to exert his own initiative.

DESIGN NO. 15

Design No. 15

CIRCULAR mirror frame, for nine-inch mirror. This is an adaptation of first lesson work. By deepening parting tool cuts to outside and bevelling toward mirror, a graceful moulded effect is obtained.

The outside diameter of this frame is 15¼″, that of the inside border is 10″, and that of the inside circle for the mirror is 8½″. The bevel toward the mirror measures ¾″. It is necessary to form a rebate (or rabbet) next to the opening on the back to hold the mirror. In this case the width is ½″ and the depth about ⅜″. This leaves room to spare for backing the mirror. Keep in mind the bevel on the face of the frame. Do not carve the rebate any deeper than necessary. This can be cut with the parting tool and large flat gouge.

The same measurements apply to Design No. 16.

DESIGN NO. 16

Design No. 16

MIRROR frame the same size as Design No. 15. This type of cutting is good training. When carving is completed, slope the back of each point to a comparatively thin edge. This makes good wall shadows instead of a solid mass.

DESIGN NO. 18

Design No. 18

Book Ends

FOLLOW the parting tool lines as shown, shallow from base and deepening to outer edges.

With the ⅝″ gouge cut on concave side of the parting tool cuts, about two-thirds across each section. Slope the opposite side away with the large flat gouge. This is a good place to try using the large flat gouge hollow side down.

The base leaf is hollowed on the base side, giving a better relief.

Slope away points at intersection of hollows and slope. This catches light.

When enlarging this design and others of this nature, try to maintain the same balance in the proportions.

DESIGN NO. 19

Design No. 19

Book Ends

THIS design shows a similar treatment to the previous example, with the exception of the scroll at the top leaf. Notice that this is rounded over.

The base is slightly rounded at the ends, and to meet the bottom parting tool cut.

Design No. 29 shows a method of support for these book ends.

DESIGN NO. 20

Design No. 20

Mirror Frame

THIS shows an application of Design No. 3.

Philippine Mahogany is used in the example, and the carving around the frame is the same used in Design No. 3.

The bevel around the mirror opening is cut with the large, flat gouge.

The advantage of this frame, if not too large, is that it can be cut out of one piece, top ornament included. If necessary, this can be done by allowing a slight reduction in the original measurement of Design No. 3.

In carving the top ornament, cut straight across the line at the upper edge of the frame proper, using the parting tool, and tilting it so that the edge of the frame is square cut. Slope away the ornament, using the large flat gouge, and carry the slope to the bottom of the parting tool cut. Draw in the details of the half rosette, and cut around the outline with the parting tool. Hollow the petals with the 5⁄8″ gouge, and the center of the ball with the same tool. Shape the leaves as shown, using the 5⁄8″ gouge for hollows. Bevel off the opposite edge with the large flat gouge.

The rebate for the mirror should be about 3⁄8″ x 3⁄8″.

DESIGN NO. 21

Design No. 21

Footstool

A SIMPLY constructed footstool is shown in the accompanying plate. The two side rails having been outlined as shown, draw the outline of the scrolls and panel above. The panel corresponds in width to the end pieces.

Cut around the scrolls with the parting tool and with the ⅝″ gouge follow the concave side of the parting tool cuts. The plate showing the partly completed piece will make this clear. Then round over the opposite side with the large flat gouge. Notice how the ⅝″ gouge cut continues from the two large scrolls along the length of the rail. The triangle formed between the upper ends of the scrolls in the panel is made with three parting tool cuts intersecting.

The stool top is moulded on the edge to what is generally termed a thumb mould. This can be made more easily with a plane than the carving tools. The gouge cutting along the thumb mould is done with the ⅜″ gouge. First divide both sides and ends into four sections. Next start on a gradual shallow curve from the top, deepening as you reach the edge of the round. This edge is very effective, catching the play of light well from any direction. The sets of gouge cuts should always be in pairs for the best effect. Sometimes a 1-inch hole is bored in the center of the top, and a four-petal rosette carved around the hole. Some prefer this finger lift.

The construction on this stool is simple and yet very workman-like. The end rails are butted between the sides, and wood pegs are driven into holes bored on an angle to each other. The top is fixed down with pocket screws. These, for the benefit of the uninitiated, consist of holes a little larger than the thickness of the screws, bored from the top of the rail and pointing out at about two inches down on the inside of the rail. Next with a $\frac{5}{8}''$ gouge, cut from the place where the drill or bit pointed through, on a deepening hollow, to a point about $\frac{3}{4}$ of an inch from the top. The screw is then entered and there is room for the screwdriver to turn in the gouge hollow.

The size of this footstool and the one following depends upon individual preference.

Design No. 22

Footstool

THE footstool plate shows the dowel construction. The rails have purposely been left open to make this clear. This piece is planned for a wood top, but if upholstery is desired, a rebate can be cut around the top edge of rails and legs to take the thickness of upholstery material. The legs are turned on a lathe, and the fluting shown is done with the ⅜″ gouge, No. 7. Observe that the flutes are tapered in proportion to match the taper of leg. This should present no difficulty at this stage.

The design on the rails is effective and comparatively simple.

First, follow the longitudinal lines with the parting tool, keeping the cut quite shallow. Deep cuts here disturb the continuity of the design. Next, make parting tool cuts separating each member, in this case at one-inch intervals. Then cut back toward the top, deepening abruptly toward the end as shown in the second last cut. This avoids the risk of bruising the border, as has already been mentioned previously. Still using the parting tool, cut from either side of the deepened parting tool cut, at the top, then with the large, flat gouge, smooth over the slopes, making the gothic arch as shown.

For the central cut, start from the top, a little clear of the top of the arch, using the parting tool, and deepening quickly to about 3/16″, then maintain that depth to the bottom line. Make the two

DESIGN NO. 22

side cuts at the bottom, as shown, then change to the ⅝″ gouge, sloping the cut inward, toward center, doing both sides in this way, and being sure to keep the gouge at an angle to the grain while cutting.

Clean decisive cutting is extremely important in a design of this type.

DESIGN NO. 23

Design No. 23

Method of Hinging and Attaching Paper for Guest-Book Covers

DESIGN No. 23 shows the inside view of guest-book covers where a more finished effect is desired, than in the rawhide strips mentioned previously.

A wood strip is glued and secured with wood pegs to the back cover, and then hinged, using brass hinges.

Some of the pages have been left loose to show the method of tying them into the covers. Holes are made part way into the inside of the back strip, and the string is doubled. A little glue is placed in the hole and a small peg glued and driven in, over the doubled string. Notice that the center strings are twice the number of each end. The strings are tied neatly inside the doubled pages.

DESIGN NO. 24

Design No. 24

THIS design is particularly suitable for a guest-book cover.

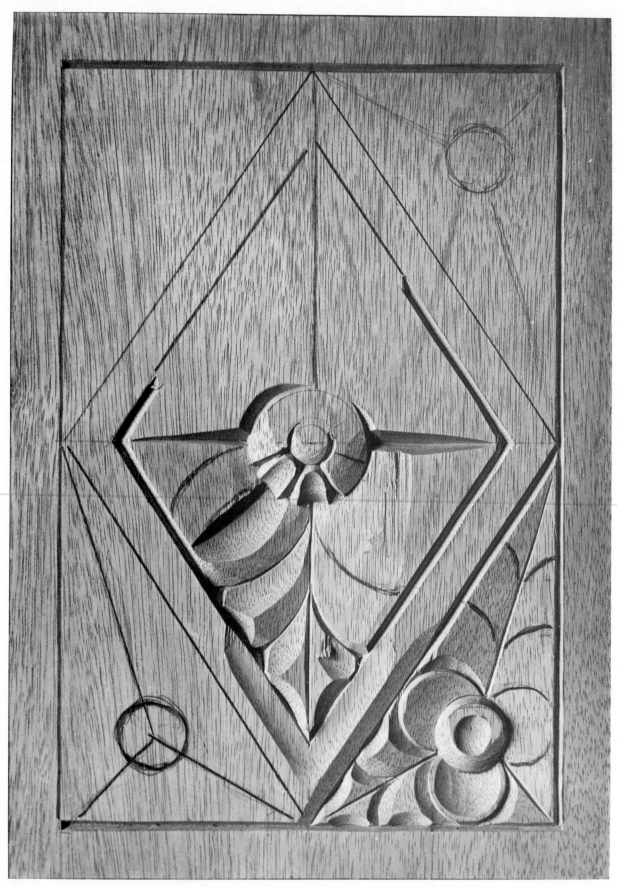

DESIGN NO. 25

Design No. 25

IN this panel there is no flat background, but a fine effect is achieved by first outlining the borders and center circles. The cuts around the circles are quite deep. The straight parting tool cuts running to the centers are started shallow, short of the points, and deepen gradually to the center.

Next, slope away three sides of the triangle corners, and four sides of the diamond, applying the design as shown. By observing the cuts in the panel shown in the photograph of this design, it will be quite obvious which tools are used.

DESIGN NO. 26

Design No. 26

AN interesting diaper pattern. The beginning is simply diagonal parting tool lines at parallel intervals. Diamonds with ball center are sloped toward the ball, remaining high at the outside edge. The others are high at the center, sloping downward to outside cut. Observe carefully the center treatment occupying the space of four smaller diamonds. This prevents monotony.

When first carving this design, prepare a panel large enough to avoid cramped workmanship.

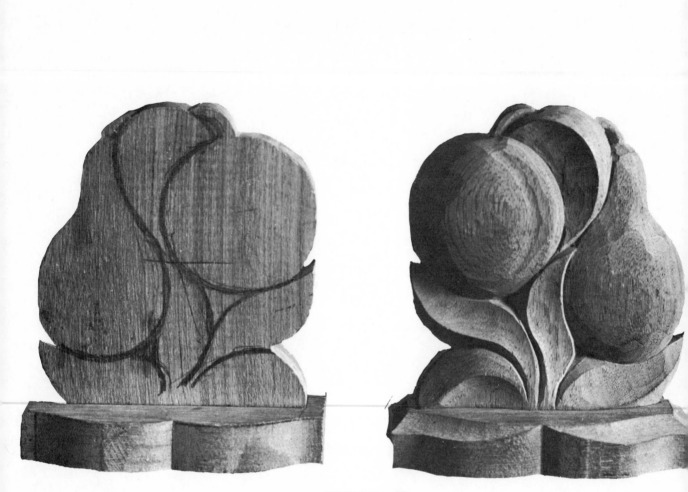

DESIGN NO. 27

Design No. 27

BOOK ends. These are six inches high, with applied base. Holes are bored in the bases and molten lead poured in, thus giving stability. The bases are, of course, applied after carving.

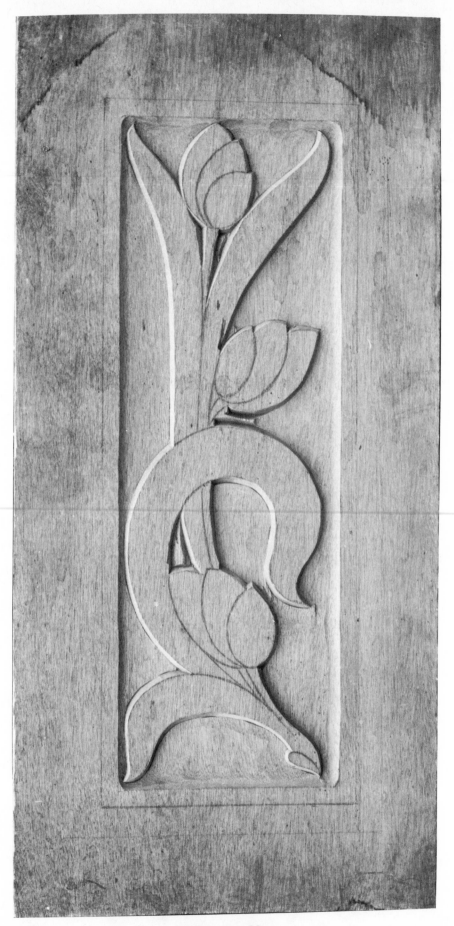

DESIGN NO. 28A

Design No. 28A

This design shows relief carving suitable for panels in cabinets or doors. Design No. 28B is the mirror image of 28A, demonstrating how such designs can be carved on panels as opposing pairs. Where appropriate, this treatment achieves a pleasing balance.

The panelled effect is obtained by cutting around the outer line with the parting tool, then with the 5⁄8″ gouge, hollowing on an angle down to the bottom of the parting tool cut. Do not cut beyond the center line. Room must be left for the center margin. Design 28B shows how this is done and the effect when finished.

The carved design is then placed inside, leaving a margin of flat surface between the fielding and the carving.

The size of this particular panel is 1″ x 29″ x 14½″, and the wood is Philippine Mahogany.

The method of treatment for carving should need no explanation at this stage. The two panels shown are self-evident.

DESIGN NO. 28B

Design No. 28B

This design shows relief carving suitable for panels in cabinets or doors. Design No. 28B is the mirror image of 28A, demonstrating how such designs can be carved on panels as opposing pairs. Where appropriate, this treatment achieves a pleasing balance.

The panelled effect is obtained by cutting around the outer line with the parting tool, then with the ⅝″ gouge, hollowing on an angle down to the bottom of the parting tool cut. Do not cut beyond the center line. Room must be left for the center margin. Design 28B shows how this is done and the effect when finished.

The carved design is then placed inside, leaving a margin of flat surface between the fielding and the carving.

The size of this particular panel is 1″ x 29″ x 14½″, and the wood is Philippine Mahogany.

The method of treatment for carving should need no explanation at this stage. The two panels shown are self-evident.

DESIGN NO. 29

Design No. 29

Conventional Wave Book Ends

THE carving in this case is exactly similar to scrolls practiced in previous lessons, so it is unnecessary to go into the details of execution. Watch the fine swing of line, and the inside finish of the scrolls. These catch the eye. The sharp edges at the back of the book ends should be removed, giving a slightly rounded effect.

A piece of stiff copper sheeting, slightly rebated into the base, makes an ample support. This should be the width of the book ends and about 3 inches the other way, making it wide enough for two or three books to rest on the copper sheeting, and insure them from tipping over.

To avoid any abrasive effect from the copper, the bottom of the sheeting can be covered with adhesive felt.

DESIGN NO. 30

Design No. 30

GUEST-BOOK cover design. This is an example of careful drawing and proportion, giving an effect of extreme simplicity, but really requiring highly skilled craftsmanship.

Notice that the border outline is done with the small gouge instead of the parting tool. This makes a softer shadow, and leads the eye to the main design.

DESIGN NO. 31

Design No. 31

ANOTHER treatment of conventional tulip design. Note the center leaf, and the effect of completely encircling the stem, yet the background is quite shallow.

DESIGN NO. 32

Design No. 32

Mirror Frame with Half-Circle Top

THIS frame brings in a different type of design. The rosettes have overlapping petals, and the leaves between have different levels, requiring more skill in execution than the previous examples. The original is 3 inches wide and 4 inches at the bottom, the extra inch for the shelf. Before applying this design to the frame, become familiar with the cuts on a practice panel.

Having shaped the outline as shown, cut lightly, about ⅛ inch deep, around the borders with the parting tool, cutting always on the side of the pencil line next to the design, leaving the borders intact. Circle the rosettes with the parting tool at the same depth, and follow the outline of the complete leaf at that depth also.

Next cut around center ball of the rosette at about ¼ inch depth, and with the large gouge slope the surrounding wood to the bottom of the ball cut. Draw in the petals, and outline with the ⅝" gouge, then using the same tool, hollow the petals, deepening to one side, as shown. Round over the center ball, using the ⅝" gouge, hollow side down.

Having completed the rosettes, proceed with the leaves. Lower the half leaves to the bottom of the parting tool cut. The ⅜" gouge will be best for this. Next hollow the complete leaves, dipping lower at either end. The same holds good for the half leaves, but of course being at a lower level they appear to dip beneath the other. Use care in keeping the effect of continuous line. There is no flat background. The small triangles are cut with three sloping cuts of the parting tool intersecting. Be sure not to cut too steeply, or it will be difficult to get a clean finish. Judge the angle so that the cuts meet, leaving no roughness.

Where the top ornament meets the frame proper, follow the line, cutting deeply with the parting tool. Then slope the ornament down with the large flat gouge to meet the bottom of that cut. Draw in the detail. Treat the two rosettes as in the border design. Outline the leaves with the parting tool, then hollow with the ⅝" gouge, sloping away the under side of the two leaves at each end, and dipping the points to a lower level. The central top piece is lowered to the level of the parting tool cut, then the inner curve is made with the ⅝" gouge. Next, slope from the extreme upper edge to the bottom of that cut, using the ⅝" gouge, and making a hollow slope. Then treat the lower part in the same way.

The two leaves on either side of the center almost form a scroll. Hollow on the inner sides with the ⅝" gouge, until the leaf begins to make the return curve. Switch to the other side and hollow to the point. Then with the large flat gouge slope the sides opposite the hollow, meeting in a center ridge.

Bevel the inner edge of the frame next to the mirror opening, using the large flat gouge and reaching a depth of about ¼ inch. Bevel only the two sides and around the circle. The bottom edge is left square and the shelf comes flush. The outer edge is rounded over from the original parting tool cut. This and the inner bevel relieve the flatness of the object.

The shelf is about 4 inches wide at the center, and is a flat curve. On the curved edge, cut two parting tool cuts a little over ⅜ of an inch apart, then with the ⅜″ gouge turned upside down make the ridge between into a bead. Then bevel off slightly both top and bottom edges.

Here, as in Design No. 15, it is necessary to form a rebate on the back next to the opening to hold the mirror.

DESIGN NO. 33

Design No. 33

CONVENTIONAL thistle. There is no flat background. Varying depths of parting tool and gouge cuts bring the whole design into strong relief.

A shallow parting tool cut is made around the two circles, and followed with a deeper cut around the outline of the thistle, proper. The main center vein of each leaf is cut quite deeply, but varying somewhat. Then both sides of these two veins are sloped away with the large flat gouge. The ⅝" gouge is then used, and occasionally the ⅜", to hollow the leaves from the center toward the border. It will be noticed that the gouge cuts vary in depth, and that the greater depth is generally at the outer edges. Parting tool cuts should then be made as shown in the accompanying plate.

The upper portion of the thistle, proper, is first sloped away to both sides, and toward the spikes, then cut at the border with the parting tool, the sharp corners being rounded off with the gouges. Gouge and parting tool cuts, as shown, complete that portion. Avoid regularity.

Round over the pod, slightly, and cut with the parting tool on lines shown. Then, with the flat gouge, slope away both lower sides of each spike. The ⅜" gouge is used between the two outer circles, sloping down toward the outer line.

DESIGN NO. 34

Design No. 34

HOLY Water font, about eighteen inches high.

This piece is shown to give an idea of the application of similiar details shown elsewhere.

One should not attempt this until quite expert.

Doors and Their Treatment

CLOSE inspection of the frontispiece of this book will show that this is the usual type of six-panel pine door, to which raised panels have been applied, slightly smaller than existing panels. Simple conventional motifs have been used, and the raised moulding around the original panels has had the beading made more interesting with a form of ball and bead cut. Plain plank doors can be made more attractive and interesting by the use of a simple design well above center.

To Make Work Bench

Materials

6 pieces of 2" x 4" - - 36" long.
2 pieces of 2" x 12" - - 48" long.
4 pieces of 1" x 4" - - 24" long.
1 lb. eightpenny box nails.
1 lb. tenpenny box nails.

Lay two 2" x 4"s on edge, and nail one of the 1" x 4"s flush with one end, using eightpenny box nails. Mark about six inches up from other end, and above that nail the other. Do the same with the other 2" x 4"s. These form the legs of the bench.

Set same on end, and nail 2" x 12"s down to same, allowing the ends to overhang frame about two inches. Tenpenny nails are used for this. Cut 2" x 4"s on angle to run from bottom 1" x 4", and to meet under center of the bench top.

This makes a practical bench, solid and yet not clumsy. The length can be varied according to conditions.

Woods Suitable for Wood Carving

Walnut

WALNUT is undoubtedly one of the finest woods available for carving, although somewhat hard cutting for a beginner, and a softer wood has advantages in the early stages.

The use of a mallet will frequently be necessary, but the sheen left from sharp tools makes finishing a pleasure. I feel that walnut should be left in its natural coloring. Linseed oil will darken it somewhat; wax scarcely affects the tone. Either makes a good finish, but for table tops, or any piece subject to hard usage, and likely to have liquids spilled on them, the oil is preferable.

Because of its fine tough grain, walnut can be used for small details and thin undercut edges. It is used for gunstocks, and cases for surgical instruments, having a noncorrosive effect on steel.

Oxalic acid can be used to bleach walnut to a lighter tone, if desired.

Oak

There are many varieties of American oak. Some are very good carving woods. Swamp oak is mostly too coarse fibered for carving, and the grain is so prominent that it mars the design. The better kinds are usually mountain growth, and one can, as a rule, get a better choice in the Eastern states. Siberian oak, commonly termed

Japanese oak, is, when selected, a very fine carving stock. Almost any lumber will vary in degrees of hardness, and what the old craftsmen term "Kindliness."

For strong, bold designs, oak is ideal, and certain varieties are good for fine detail. Oak has been sneered at, not through any fault of the wood, but because of the dreadful finishes of the golden-oak period. Personally, I feel that each wood should be left as nearly as possible under its own hallmark. I do not mean to imply that it cannot be stained, but that the pores should not be filled. Why make a wood to look like metal or stone? Again, it should not be necessary to wait fifty years for a piece to soften or mature, if one can get the desired effect right away.

Nearly all of the oaks react to ammonia, and this liquid, preferably concentrated, will darken the wood, as it would age naturally. Fumed oak, popular some years ago, was simply the piece, or pieces of oak placed in an air-tight box or room with some shallow vessels of concentrated ammonia. Usually a sample of the same wood was placed where it could be withdrawn, to note the darkening. A wash of concentrated ammonia will give a good tone, but let me caution you to use rubber gloves, and keep well to the windward side. Should you not be sure which side is windward or leeward, you'll never have a better opportunity of finding out, and you won't forget the lesson when the tears stop streaming.

Should this application not darken the wood sufficiently, a second will sometimes help, and if a still darker tone is desired, use some of the walnut stain. The method of making the walnut stain will be found under the heading *Stains and Finishes*. Should that not be practicable for you, a good walnut water stain in powder form can be bought at a good paint store, and boiled in water.

Ordinary sal soda is sometimes used with good effect on oak. It is well to wash the surface off with cold, clean water after this treatment. Otherwise there is a powdery deposit which may make for difficulty in finishing.

Many prefer simply a wax finish on oak. I agree on most objects, except table tops, when an oil finish is, I think, superior, although many of the commercial paste wax products are quite good. The beeswax and turpentine preparation is explained under the chapter on stains and finishes.

Teakwood

Many make the mistake of thinking teakwood is always black, and very hard with a harsh grain. This error arises through the fact that the Chinese teak is a red, harsh-grained wood, and is generally dyed to a blackish tone.

The Burma or Siam teak is a comparatively soft wood; medium hard would better express it. It is of a lovely deep fawny tone with darker stripes occasionally, and when freshly cut, is almost green in coloring. This wood is used for the decks of ships sailing mostly in tropical waters, and is practically unaffected by heat or cold. In other words, it does not shrink or swell nearly as much as most woods, and because of its natural oily quality, is more lasting than almost any other wood, even when unpainted.

One of the drawbacks is that Burma teak dulls tools rapidly, supposedly the oil affecting the steel, because the wood itself is easily cut, and many grades have no grit.

An old wood carver once told me that if one can keep a dish of water handy and dip the tools frequently, the cutting edge will be preserved longer, but I'd sooner sharpen oftener; it is less bother.

Teakwood can be finished with wax or oil, and the natural coloring left, as the wood itself will darken to a light chocolate brown.

Difficulty will sometimes be experienced in gluing up teak, and to prevent trouble, a solution of sal soda and hot water is sometimes used on the joints before gluing up, this being followed by a wash of clean hot water, and of course, allowed to dry thoroughly before the glue is applied.

Philippine Mahogany

This is not really a true mahogany, and has frequently been derided, but in many cases undeservedly. Very often this wood has been employed in cheap furniture, inferior grades, and cheap finishes, combinations that would lower the rating of any wood.

There are a great many varieties of this lumber, ranging from what is known as white to dark red. For beginners work, yes, even for professional, I prefer the classification of light red. If the wood is to be carved, it should be free, as far as possible from ribbon grain. A large percentage of this wood carves very nicely, and has the important feature of being not too hard for a beginner.

Philippine mahogany loses its color when exposed to light for any period of time, so I always make a practice of bleaching before staining, thus preventing any change in the wood tone afterwards. Clorox, or any good commercial bleach can be used. Ammonia will also act as a bleach on this wood. Hot lime and lye can be used for a light finish, or simply wax after the bleaching. Water stains can be used if darker tones are desired.

Ponderosa Pine

This wood, when selected, is very fine for smaller articles. Choose the white, silky boards, not those with strong grain. Pine does not react well to water stains. I usually apply a stain made with umber or sienna, raw or burnt. Use burnt umber if you want the redder tones, mixed to the consistency of milk with gasoline or solvent.

Apply stain with a brush, rub off surplus with a rag, following the grain, and when dry, wax. Leave wax on for about twenty minutes, then polish. A stiff, cheap nail or scrub brush is ideal for polishing the carvings. More wax can be applied if desired.

Sugar Pine

This wood is more porous than Ponderosa pine, the good grade being very fine for many types of carving.

Mahogany

West Coast: Thus described because it is from the west coast of South America, this is a rich-grained hardwood. Some of it carves quite nicely, but much of it is too grainy and splinters readily.

Honduras Mahogany: This wood, much used by pattern makers, is soft and nice cutting. While usually a finer grain, it is in many cases not much harder than Philippine mahogany.

Santo Domingo Mahogany is very hard and richly grained. It is now rare. It is not ideal for carving.

Cuban Mahogany has a dense grain and varies in hardness. Most of this mahogany is good for carving.

Spanish Cedar

This is not a true cedar, but is familiar to the layman as such in that it was used altogether at one time for cigar boxes. It has an agreeable aroma and is a favorite of pattern makers. It varies in texture, and most of it is good for carving. This wood is much used in Mexico for frames, statues, etc.

Lime or Linden

The British lime tree, or the Continental linden, is what one might term an ideal wood, especially for carving in the round. Grinling Gibbons, the famous English wood carver, favored this wood above all others, and many of the old wood-carved figures were in this wood. Creamy white in color, and easily cut, the grain is practically negligible, so that one can cut across the end wood with ease.

Southern Red Gum

A fine carving wood, being the heart wood of the tree. The sap-wood is sold as white gum, and is not good for carving purposes. Gum was formerly guilty of warping and twisting badly. But with improved methods of cutting, quartered, I believe, this tendency has been mostly eliminated.

Boxwood

Boxwood is very hard, dense in grain, deep yellow in color, and is ideal for wood blocks and smaller objects. It is sold by the pound, and is too expensive to use for large objects, and is seldom found in large pieces.

Basswood

This is light, soft, white in color, and is suitable for objects not subject to wear and tear.

Apple

Applewood makes good carving, taking a nice finish.

Olive

Olive is a fine carving wood, with a rich green-brown color. It is splendid for fine detail work.

Ebony

Ebony is black, is ideal for small carvings, is difficult to obtain in large pieces, and is expensive.

Lignum Vitae

This is a very heavy, hard, and strong-grained wood, greenish brown to near black in color. It makes hard cutting, usually for small objects, and is expensive.

Rosewood, Brazilian

Rosewood is rich grained, reddish brown with almost yellow and black streaks, carves nicely, and is expensive.

Yellow Poplar

This is usually comparatively soft, but not easy to cut, as it seems to grip the tools. The coloring is from a cream to a light green when freshly cut, but on exposure turns a dirty brown. It is too soft for hard wear and tear, as it bruises readily.

Siberian Birch

When selected, this wood has a very fine consistency, and is of an ivory white tone, and quite hard.

American Birch

There are several varieties of this wood, mostly good for carving, and usually hard.

Maple

Maple is quite hard, and usually does not lend itself to carving.

Holly

This is difficult to obtain in size or quantity.

Pear Tree

This is good carving wood, as are most fruit trees.

Magnolia

Requires hard cutting, but stands up well.

Myrtle

Myrtle is a good carving wood, but is usually difficult to obtain in any quantity.

Cherry

This is used generally for fine carving, and is a good furniture wood.

Preliminary Method of Preparing Woods for Finishing

THIS chapter is written for the beginner in finishing, and will be followed by the more advanced methods.

For schools and before one becomes expert, sandpapering across the grain should be avoided.

Oil stains are simple, and give quite good results, though they do not come up to the standard of the water stains for a high-class finish. There are many good commercial stains on the market.

In the advanced chapter, I advocate staining and finishing parts of chairs, and certain other pieces, before assembling. This might present too many problems for the inexperienced, therefore the assembling should be done before staining.

Advanced Methods of Preparing Woods for Finishing

FINISHING of panels or articles is as important as the design or carving. Many otherwise good pieces are ruined by incompetent finishing, varnishes, shellac, poor stains, etc.

The different woods have to be considered, and let me caution you that sandpapering can destroy good wood carving, bringing it into the same class as machine carving and sandblasting.

Take, for example, a chest. Having completed the carving and assembled the piece (I find it better to assemble a chest before finishing; chairs, dining tables, benches, etc., in most cases are more easily stained and finished before assembling), proceed to sandpaper as follows:

On a large, flat surface such as the chest lid, use No. 180. This applies to the carborundum sandpapers, black surfaced. They do not scratch or tear the wood as will the ordinary sandpapers. Halve a sheet by folding the surfaces together and tearing cleanly down the center. A half sheet should then be folded once, cutting sides out, and placed over a sandpaper block or cork. I advocate a piece of cork about three inches wide, four or five inches long, and about two or two and one-half inches thick. Rub the cork down level on the side to be used and fold the sandpaper over it so the edges can be held with the finger and thumb. Where a smooth level surface is desired, first sand straight across the grain. This will remove, or almost so, the undulations left by the smoothing plane. Here let me mention that I detest machine-sanded surfaces. The grain rises continually, and the wood loses the sheen and life given by a sharp plane. Also don't try to finish directly when the wood is machine planed, for the whole surface will show the slight ripple left by the cutters. From the beginning bear in mind that a finish that will last and grow old beautifully, is in the wood, not on it. Therefore avoid spray guns, lacquers, and varnishes.

When the first sanding is complete, take No. 100 sandpaper and proceed to sandpaper *with* the grain, taking care to erase completely all the marks left by the first sanding across the grain. Be sure to dust off the surface occasionally, and knock the dust off the sandpaper. When satisfied with the second process, again take No. 180 and sandpaper with the grain. The sandpaper can be folded differently as it wears. Be sure never to leave marks of sandpapering across the grain, especially when water stains are to be used, but at no time is it a good practice. The surface should now be like satin to the touch. My definition of a finished surface, as explained to my apprentices, is that when a fly tries to alight on it, he skids off and breaks his neck. When the finished surface has reached that stage, it can safely be called good.

The next step is to take a clean rag, preferably linen, with fairly warm water, and lightly dampen the surface all over. When dry, any grain that may have been crushed, will rise up and can be removed by sanding lightly with the grain, using worn No. 180, without the sandpaper block. The methods of bleaching and staining, etc., will be found under the chapter dealing with the different woods.

The carved surfaces should not be sandpapered. My usual procedure is to use a piece of worn No. 180, and lightly, with the grain, rub the high, sharp edges. This softens the surfaces, and holds the light better. Do not dampen carving. If the tools have been conditioned properly, and used properly, the grain will not be crushed.

Stains and Finishes

Walnut Stain

A GOOD walnut stain can be made by crushing black walnuts, green or otherwise, and placing in an airtight jar, covering the pulp with a concentrated ammonia, and leaving for some weeks, if possible. The liquid, when poured off, is ready for use, but some boiling water can be poured over the remaining pulp and stirred up; this resulting liquid can be added to the first, then the whole poured through a fine strainer.

Beeswax and Turpentine

Melt a quantity of beeswax in a tin, remove from the flame, and stir in turpentine. It will be necessary to experiment with the quantity of turpentine to be added. When the whole is cold, it should be in the form of a fairly stiff paste, and can be kept in a sealed container. Some advocate the addition of a small piece of paraffin wax. This is optional.

Some prefer to put the first coating of wax on hot, especially for table tops. It has a more penetrating effect. The surplus should be rubbed off as the wax cools, or it will pile up and give a great deal of unnecessary labor afterwards. The wax can be applied with a pad of 000 steel wool. This will prevent the wax from piling up.

Bichromate of Potash

This stain will darken mahogany (real mahogany), giving the same tone as age. The liquid can be used strong or weak, depending on depth of tone required. The crystals, obtained at a drug-store, are simply dissolved in water. Bichromate of Potash can be liquefied more rapidly by boiling. Should the crystals not be fully dissolved, add more water. Successive coats can be applied should a darker tone be desired. So do not judge the color when dry, but have a small sample piece. After stain has dried, apply linseed oil. This shows the finished shade.

The objection to the use of this treatment is that if the wood is red, the potash simply deepens the red tone; therefore if a brown finish is desired, one of the other stains must be used.

Lye

Dissolved in boiling water, lye will give an antique tone to many woods. Care should be used, and rubber gloves worn for protection of the hands. Brushes are of little use, as they disintegrate rapidly. A cloth on the end of a stick suits the purpose.

Hot Lime

Hot lime is often used for antique effects. Slake the lime by pouring water over it, taking care to keep adding water, as the lime will burn and lose effect. Add water until the whole forms a paste. Care should be taken not to handle the lime, as serious burns may result. During the process of slaking, be careful not to get close to the steam. Cover the article to be finished with this paste, then before the paste dries, wash the whole off with clear cold water.

Lye and Hot Lime are sometimes used together, resulting in a good effect. Only wax should be used for a finish after lye, or hot lime treatment, as oil darkens.

Black Asphaltum Varnish

A good stain for cheaper woods can be made from black asphaltum. This is really a varnish for metal. But by using a small quantity in a liberal quantity of gasoline or solvent, a brown stain results. Varied effects can be obtained by adding color pigments. White lead, for instance, gives a creamy brown, while greens, reds, yellows may be used as desired.

Other Finishes

For a finish that is quicker than the usual procedure followed with linseed oil, I recommend the following:

Having followed the directions for sanding, bleaching if necessary, and staining—and while I think of it—be sure to sand between all stages, using worn 180, and no sandpaper block. By doing this, you keep the surfaces satiny, and final process is simplified, and the result more satisfactory.

When the stain—I allude here to water stains—is partly dry, slightly dampen a rag with bleaching liquid, and carefully lighten the raised portions of the carving. This will bring out the details, and relieve the whole design. Do not worry if you seem to get the raised portions too light. It will be found that they darken down partially under the finish.

When the stain is thoroughly dry, and lightly sanded, go over the whole of the work with a quick, light application of French Spirit Varnish. This is the aristocrat of the shellac families. In fact, shellac is a very poor forty-second cousin. Before applying the spirit varnish, dilute with the addition of about one-third denatured alcohol. Use a soft, broad brush, and do not work over. Flow thinly but freely, so that when dry the slight deposit is into the pores of the wood, sealing the stain. Be careful not to overlap, and when finishing edges, rub a finger lightly along the corners to prevent runs. When this first coat is dry, lightly sand. Then prepare what is known in French polishing as a "rubber."

This rubber consists of a wad of cotton batting over which a piece of worn linen or cheesecloth is stretched. Saturate with spirit varnish. Apply a second coat of spirit varnish with the brush, only doing a panel or top at a time. Take the rubber, apply a little raw linseed oil over the cloth, and commence to stroke lightly over the surface just varnished, being careful not to let the rubber stick. Use enough oil to prevent this. Keep working over the surface lightly until a sheen is obtained. Within half an hour, go over this with No. 000 steel wool, always with the grain. Linseed oil can be applied to this surface at any time, and a very satisfactory finish is the result. Wax can be used instead if desired.

For table tops, I prefer to flow the second coat of spirit varnish, and pour raw linseed oil on immediately. But it is wise to have someone follow up with the oil, as the varnish should not be allowed to dry. Leave the top with the oil pooled on it for several days, as free from dust as possible. The weather or heating condition has a great deal to do with the time, but a fair test is when the oil begins to gum a little. Remove all surplus oil, and be careful to burn rags used. They are always a fire hazard.

Rub the table top briskly, using worn flannel preferably. It will be found that for some time there will be a sweating of the oil, so it is important to rub briskly for several days. At intervals of a week or two weeks, a little oil may be applied. It is sufficient to dampen a rag, then rub hard. Always remember that your finish is in the wood, not on it, so avoid piling up surface coatings.

Machine Carving

Wood carving is undoubtedly one of the oldest of the crafts, and within the last few years is coming into its own again after many years of disrepute, at least in this country, and in Britain for many years it was confined to a few professional groups and enthusiastic amateurs.

Machine carving, as it is generally called, has, for commercial purposes, replaced hand carving, but it seldom has a worth-while value, lacking the clean-cut light and shade effect of hand carving. For the benefit of those who do not know how machine carving is done, I shall briefly describe one method.

A wood carver first carves by hand a panel, we shall say, to the design required. One type of machine has long arms extending over a bench. At intervals on the arms are drills. The center drill is blind, in other words, noncutting. Beneath this blind drill the carved panel is placed and panels of the same size are fixed beneath the active drills. A workman then guides the blind drill over the carved panel, the whole machine raising and lowering, moving backward and forward, right or left, and the active drills cut away to correspond with the original. The finish on the panels is, of course, incomplete, for the corners are all rounded, and for veins, etc., it is necessary for a carver to touch up the pieces. It requires but little skill to tell a piece of machine carving. The wood lacks the luster left by a clean-cutting chisel or gouge, and instead of the confident marks of the tool, the surfaces are indefinite and dead.